# The Ghostly Tales of Coeur d'Alene

Published by Arcadia Children's Books
A Division of Arcadia Publishing
Charleston, SC
www.arcadiapublishing.com

Copyright © 2023 by Arcadia Children's Books
All rights reserved

Spooky America is a trademark of Arcadia Publishing, Inc.

First published 2023

ISBN 978-1-5402-5779-6

Library of Congress Control Number: 2023937856

Notice: The information in this book is true and complete to the best of our knowledge. It is offered without guarantee on the part of the author or Arcadia Publishing. The author and Arcadia Publishing disclaim all liability in connection with the use of this book.

All rights reserved. No part of this book may be reproduced or transmitted in any form whatsoever without prior written permission from the publisher except in the case of brief quotations embodied in critical articles and reviews.

Images used courtesy of Shutterstock.com; pp. 6-7 Wollertz/Shutterstock.com; pp. 10, 78-79 Kirk Fisher/Shutterstock.com.

*Spooky America*

# THE GHOSTLY TALES OF COEUR D'ALENE

### DEBORAH CUYLE

Adapted from Ghosts of Coeur d'Alene and the Silver Valley by Deborah Cuyle

MONTANA

WASHINGTON

IDAHO

# Table of Contents & Map Key

Welcome to Spooky Coeur d'Alene! . . . . . . . . . . . . . 3

Part 1: Coeur d'Alene Haunts . . . . . . . . . . . . . . . . . . . . . . . . 8

Chapter 1. Coeur d'Alene . . . . . . . . . . . . . . . . . . . . . . . . . 11
1. The Roosevelt Inn
2. Downtown Coeur d'Alene
3. North Idaho College
4. Farragut State Park
5. Spirit Lake
6. The Bates Motel
7. D-Mac's

Part 2: Silver Valley Haunts . . . . . . . . . . . . . . . . . . . . . . . . 38

8. Chapter 2. The Cataldo Mission . . . . . . . . . . . . . . . . . 43

Chapter 3. Murray . . . . . . . . . . . . . . . . . . . . . . . . . . . . . 49
9. A Ghost in Search of Gold
10. The Ghost on the Stairs
11. Haunted Antiques

Chapter 4. Kellogg . . . . . . . . . . . . . . . . . . . . . . . . . . . . . 67
12. A Donkey and a Dream
13. The Sunshine Mine Disaster
14. Missing Gold

Chapter 5. Wallace . . . . . . . . . . . . . . . . . . . . . . . . . . . . 81
15. A Movie Star and Memories
16. The Ghost of Mournful Maggie
17. A "Sweet" Ghost
18. The Ryan Hotel
19. The Brooks Hotel
20. A Phantom Fireman
21. Ghosts on Stage
22. Nine Mile Cemetery

A Ghostly Goodbye . . . . . . . . . . . . . . . . . . . . . . . 107

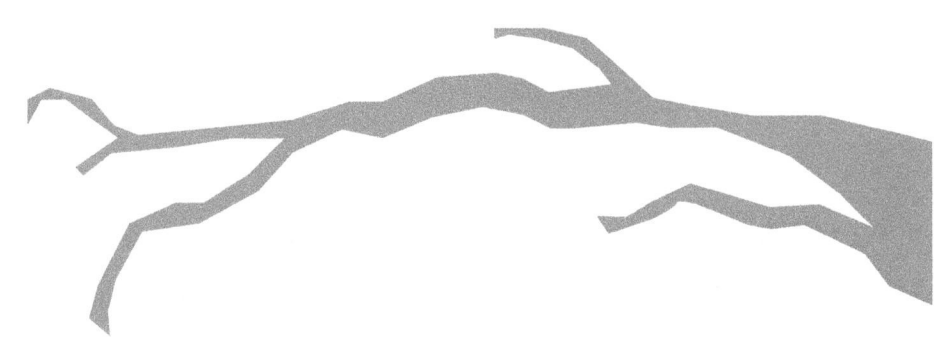

# Welcome to Spooky Coeur d'Alene!

Do you like a good scare? Do you enjoy sharing spooky stories with your friends while huddled around a campfire or nestled together at a slumber party? Well, you're in luck! The eerie tales in this book will give you a supply of spooky stories you can tell to frighten your friends!

Located in northern Idaho, the city of Coeur d'Alene is probably one of the most beautiful places in America—but also one of the scariest! Ghosts tend to linger in almost every corner of the old buildings in Coeur d'Alene. But the ghosts don't stop at the city limits! Similar creepy hauntings continue throughout the entire region known as the Silver Valley.

Most of the ghosts in this book do more than just go bump in the night. These spirits love to move objects, touch people with their invisible hands, knock on doors and walls, and even cry out their names! In downtown Coeur d'Alene, the restless spirit of a mischievous child still plays pranks on guests who stay the night at the luxurious Roosevelt Inn. During the late 1880s, a mob-style killer named Fatty plagued downtown Coeur d'Alene, and many soldiers simply *disappeared* when they crossed his path. Their skeletons were found years later by workers.

WELCOME TO SPOOKY COEUR D'ALENE!

In nearby towns, other ghosts roam the buildings and walk the streets, scaring and harassing unsuspecting citizens. The restless spirits of miners still haunt towns where the mine owners lived a life of luxury while the workers risked their lives every day to earn just pennies. Owners of several historic hotels share the eerie stories of phantom visitors: apparitions of dark figures that peer around doors and the creepy, lingering odors of cigars or perfume seemingly coming out of nowhere.

Who are these ghosts? What do they want? Why do they continue to haunt places so many years later? No one seems to know the answers to these questions...

If you love scary stories, then settle into a cozy chair and dig deeper into these strange and hair-raising tales of the ghosts and ghouls of Coeur d'Alene and the Silver Valley!

Coeur d'Alene

# Part 1: Coeur d'Alene Haunts

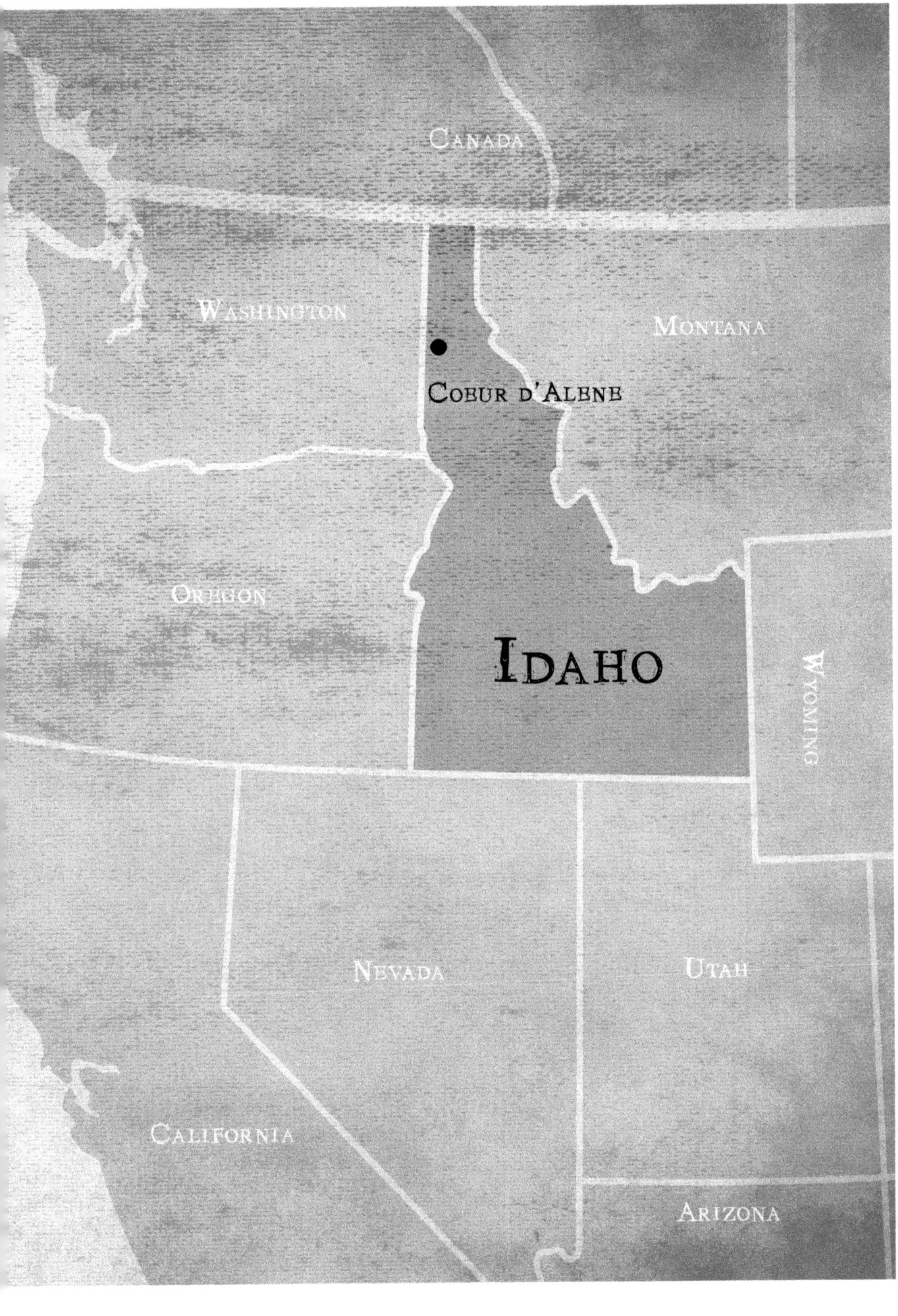

CANADA

WASHINGTON

● 
COEUR D'ALENE

MONTANA

OREGON

IDAHO

WYOMING

NEVADA

UTAH

CALIFORNIA

ARIZONA

Downtown Coeur d'Alene

# Coeur d'Alene

## The Roosevelt Inn

The Roosevelt Inn was built in 1905, and up until 1971, it served as a school for first through sixth graders. From 1971 until 1992, it became storage and office space, and in 1992, it was converted into a bed-and-breakfast. Today, it is a beautiful hotel that caters to guests who are willing to share their room with a ghost or two! The five-story brick building is nestled in downtown Coeur d'Alene, just a short walk from Lake Coeur d'Alene. The rooms are filled with Victorian-style furnishings, lace curtains, delicate stained-glass windows, and colorful, hand-painted murals. An intricate, black wrought-iron fence secures the grounds, and the sounds of trickling fountains fill guests' ears when they walk up to the entrance of the glorious hotel.

The hotel is so beautiful, it is no wonder its resident ghosts don't want to leave!

The most active ghost at the Roosevelt Inn is a little boy named Dennis. He is about seven years old and loves to play tricks on people. Once, Dennis unscrewed all of the lights from the ceiling on the third floor in the hotel. The owner, John Hough, thought the fuses had blown, causing the lights to not work. But when he discovered Dennis's prank, he did not find the joke very funny at all. He had to pull out a very tall ladder to screw the lightbulbs back in—all thirty-eight of them!

Another time, when John's wife, Tina, was baking cookies, the cabinet doors in the kitchen kept opening and closing all by themselves. Tina simply said, "Dennis, quit it!" And the cabinets remained closed for the rest of her baking session.

One of Dennis's favorite tricks is *appearing* when new guests arrive. Guests are shocked (and a little bit frightened) by the little boy's ghostly appearance as Dennis eagerly waves, welcoming them all to *his* hotel. Sometimes Dennis can be seen running from room to room, tucking behind doors and furniture as if playing hide-and-seek with an invisible friend. The guests and staff agree that while Dennis is a bit mischievous, he really just wants to laugh and play games, like any child would.

Perhaps, if you ever get to stay the night in one of the gorgeous rooms at the Roosevelt Inn, you will get the chance to see Dennis (and wave back to him!) for yourself. Maybe you'll even be lucky enough to play catch with him in the hallway!

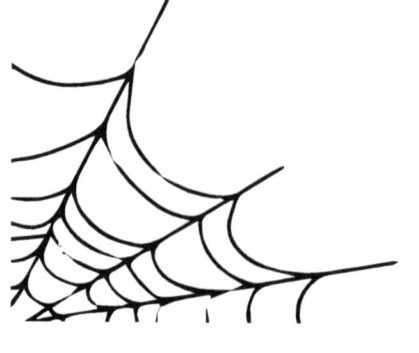

Another ghost who haunts the Roosevelt Inn is believed to be a teacher. When her spirit appears, she is typically wearing a long-sleeved, white dress, and her hair is neatly tied up in a bun. This mysterious ghost appears to be about fifty years old. Although no one knows for sure who this ghost is, many people think she is Miss Millenious, who taught at the school in the 1940s and 50s. She never has any feet when she makes an appearance and seems to float wherever she goes. And apparently, judging by the way she's known to sometimes flicker the lights, lock doors, and even rearrange furniture in the middle of the night, she is not happy about the renovations that have taken place over the years!

Miss Millenious lived in a small cottage across the street from the Roosevelt Inn, and that is where she tragically died. Perhaps she is still patrolling the hallways looking for misbehaved and unruly children? Or perhaps she is even keeping an eye on Dennis!

The owners of the inn don't seem to mind their two in-house phantom residents—in fact, they enjoy their company. Perhaps someday they'll solve the puzzle as to why these two ghosts continue to haunt the Roosevelt Inn. But regardless of who these spirits are, the guests, staff, and owners of the Roosevelt Inn seem happy to share space with the ghosts known as Dennis and Miss Millenious.

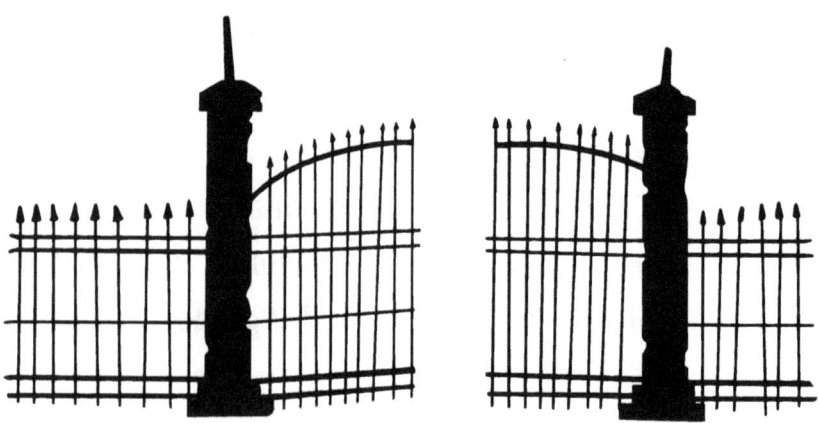

## Downtown Coeur d'Alene

Coeur d'Alene was a hard town in the early days. And one of the most feared men around was Jim Metzger, also known as Fatty Carroll. Everyone knew not to cross Fatty. If you did, you might very well end up in a shallow grave somewhere. Many believe the ghosts of his victims still haunt downtown Coeur d'Alene and nearby Fort Sherman.

In 1887, three Indigenous people disappeared from a nearby reservation and five soldiers went missing from Fort Sherman. Commanders at the fort believed the soldiers had run off and deserted their duties to the U.S. Army. No one ever found the eight men—or their bodies. Locals suspected that something terrible had happened to them.

Unfortunately, it seems the locals may have been right.

During his life, Fatty owned many buildings in Coeur d'Alene, as well as lots of land outside of town. After Fatty died, his buildings and land were sold. When workers were making improvements at one of those buildings on the corner of 4th Street and Sherman Avenue, they stumbled across a grisly sight. Digging in the exact spot where one of Fatty's businesses had been located, the workers unearthed a number of skeletons! Could these be the skeletons of the eight men who went missing from Fort Sherman? Unfortunately, the shallow graves revealed no clues, and no personal items were discovered with the bones. The town eventually

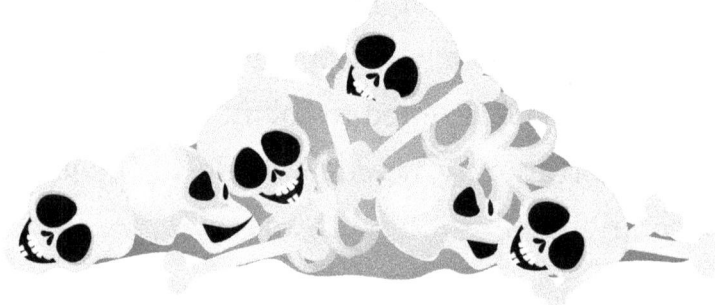

gave the bones a proper burial, but no one ever figured out who the bodies belonged to. Could the spirits of those unknown people be wandering town in search of their killer?

And those weren't the only skeletons discovered lying beneath Coeur d'Alene. Some were unearthed as recently as 2019 in an area known as Tubbs Hill. And yes, Fatty had once owned land in that area.

As far as we know, Fatty never went to jail for any of his alleged crimes. Would you believe the ghosts of his likely victims still wander the streets of Coeur d'Alene in search of Fatty Carroll and justice?

## North Idaho College

North Idaho College has more than just faculty, staff, and students on campus. At this community college located on the beautiful shores of Lake Coeur d'Alene, *ghosts* walk among the living, too! Strolling across the campus, people have been known to experience all kinds of creepy things, from the spooky sensation of being watched, to seeing strange shadows, to feeling eerie chills on warm days. (Ghost hunters believe an area of low temperature indicates the presence of a ghost.) Students and faculty report seeing the apparition of a man in an army uniform walking up and down the halls of Boswell Hall, the sound of heavy footsteps echoing as he makes his way through the building. Some say he can even walk through walls!

The source of this ghostly presence may date back all the way to the late 1800s. Impressed by the area's beauty and location, General William Sherman proposed that a military fort be built near the site where the Spokane River flows into Lake Coeur d'Alene. Today, North Idaho College is located where some of the old fort used to stand.

Soldiers who worked at the fort would sometimes go missing on payday. The men liked to walk to downtown Coeur d'Alene to play cards, dance, and have a good time. But every now and then, some of them went into town and didn't come back. When the men were absent the next morning at roll call, the rumors would start to swirl. Had the missing men gotten lost on their way back to the fort? Had they run away? Or worse: Had they been hurt... or even *killed*?

Is the spirit that people have seen and felt on campus one of those missing soldiers? Or is it General William Sherman still watching over his men and the fort? No one knows for sure, and the identity of the spooky presence remains a mystery. But whoever the ghost or ghosts may be, they seem to be taking their ghostly duties *very* seriously.

## Farragut State Park

There is more than just camping going on at Farragut State Park. Located near Athol, about twenty-five miles north of Coeur d'Alene in the beautiful Coeur d'Alene Mountains, Farragut State Park is a popular spot for camping, hiking, boating, fishing, and other outdoor activities. But many people have also had strange experiences while visiting this four-thousand-acre park. Spooky tales of moving statues, mysterious groans and moans, and sightings of ghostly prisoners are common among brave tourists and park employees.

After the Japanese bombed Pearl Harbor in 1941, the site was rebuilt as a training facility for United States Navy seamen. Almost three hundred thousand men lived and trained at this huge facility, and it was the second largest U.S. Naval training center in the world.

Around 1945, it was used as a prisoner-of-war camp, housing German soldiers the United States had captured in Europe and Africa. Ghost hunters believe the ghosts that haunt the state park are these prisoners—their spirits trapped in death where they were once confined in life.

The most haunted building in the park is the brig. (A brig is a military prison or jail.) The brig is one of the few original buildings that still stands today. It was built out of concrete blocks with twelve-foot-tall steel gates to make sure no prisoners could ever escape. (Apparently, the brig was so secure, nobody ever *did* escape—in this life or the next!) Many people have felt the touch of invisible ice-cold hands when they are walking around the brig. Others have heard strange groans and cries coming from unseen phantoms. Other people, still, claim to have had rocks thrown at them

by an unknown, invisible force. Some believe this angry ghost is probably the spirit of a German soldier who died while being held at the brig. (Records show that only one prisoner died while being held at the facility.)

Rumor says the angry and scared German soldier continues to haunt the brig because he did not receive a proper burial. No one knows if this is true or not, but one thing is certain—that ghost certainly wants to let the living world know that it's unhappy about something!

Not that far from the brig in Memorial Park stands a unique (some might even say spooky) statue. It's a bronze bust of a World War II sailor, whose eyes stare off eerily into the distance. But even *eerier*? If you look closely, you'll see his face is etched with the smaller faces of other sailors. And sometimes—either late at night or early in the morning—the faces of these soldiers carved into the stone are said to actually *move*! According to park employees, the statue is meant to represent all the people who help train sailors. Oddly, however, all those etched faces seem to have given the statue a "life" of its own. Visitors have said they feel as if they are being watched as they walk by, as if the statue's eyes are following their every move. Is this a mere trick of the light? An optical illusion? Or is something more supernatural at play?

Part of the campground is located on Lake Pend Oreille, and people have seen mysterious lights hovering over the water, accompanied by eerie sounds and shadowy figures. Hikers and campers have told stories of these bizarre phenomena for many years. What are the lights? Where (or what) are the strange sounds coming from? Are the shadowy figures ghosts or something else?

Haunted or not, if you ever get the chance to visit Farragut State Park, be sure to keep your eyes and ears open. From the strange to the otherworldly, you never know what you may encounter.

## Spirit Lake

The small town of Spirit Lake has many ghostly spirits! Established in 1908 and about twenty-five miles north of Coeur d'Alene, it was often referred to as the handsomest little town in northern Idaho. The Indigenous people who lived in the area called the body of water Lake Kaniskee, which means Lake of the Spirit.

A local legend says the ghost of a beautiful girl haunts the lake. She was in love with a boy from her tribe, but her tribe had arranged for her to marry a boy from another tribe. The marriage was to help make peace between the tribes. The couple who was in love couldn't bear the thought of being apart, so they rowed a canoe out into the middle of Spirit Lake, where they dove into the water, never to be seen again.

Though the two were never found, local folklore says that on moonlit nights when the wind is calm and the water still, you can see the ghostly silhouette of a couple in their canoe, drifting across the lake. Are these the spirits of the girl and boy? Or perhaps the ghosts of their heartbroken parents still searching for their

lost children? Whoever the ghosts may be, it appears they may be drifting across the lake for all eternity.

Another Spirit Lake legend involves an old silver prospector who lived as a hermit on the water's edge in the late 1800s. He was always looking for silver and gold, hoping to one day strike it rich. Day after day, he looked for his fortune but never found any valuable nuggets.

Soon the old man became frustrated and depressed. Legend claims he burned his cabin

to the ground and then tragically took his own life.

To this day, early morning risers might just catch a glimpse of the prospector's restless spirit at the water's edge, hunched over, looking into the lake for shiny objects that might possibly turn out to be silver or gold.

Yet another legend is told of an old spirit named Amotkan who ruled over Spirit Lake. Indigenous people who lived near the lake

believed that Amotkan became angry at them and decided to dry up the lake as punishment. Without the lake, people could not fish, and some began to starve to death.

One day, a young wolf came out from the woods in search of water to drink. When he found out about Amotkan's cruel curse, the wolf vowed to save the lake people from starvation. Late one night, the wolf crept up on Amotkan while he was sleeping and killed him. The death of Amotkan released the villagers from the spell, and the lake began to refill with water.

The lake people were saved!

If you get a chance to visit Spirit Lake, perhaps you'll also meet one of the spirits that gives this beautiful but eerie place its name... and learn for *yourself* why these crystal blue waters are considered among the most haunted in Idaho.

## The Bates Motel

You may have heard of the horror movie *Psycho*. It was directed by the legendary movie director Alfred Hitchcock and contains a *very* scary shower scene. Most of the movie takes place at the Bates Motel, and the movie and newer TV series with that name are based on that spooky place.

The Bates Motel in Coeur d'Alene is not connected to the movies or TV shows—but that doesn't mean Coeur d'Alene's motel doesn't have its fair share of scary happenings! The motel is located on Sherman Avenue and of its thirteen rooms, #1 and #3 are reportedly the most haunted. Guests and staff report pockets of cold air in those rooms even during the summer, towels being moved as if by invisible hands, lights turning on and off by themselves, and the spine-tingling sensation of being watched when no one else is in the room.

The building did not begin as a motel. It was originally a barracks for soldiers during World War II. Once the war was over, the building was turned into a motel called the Roadway Inn. A few years later, a man named Randy Bates purchased the motel and named it after himself. Little did he know how infamous (and infamously spooky) his motel would become!

It's said that Robert Bloch, the author of the horror novel *Psycho* (the book upon which the movie and TV show are based), stayed at the Bates Motel in 1959, and his eerie experiences as a guest there are partly what inspired his creepy novel. But what happened to Mr. Bloch while he stayed at the Bates Motel? What could have scared him so much that he ended up writing such a bone-chilling tale?

We may never know for sure, but what we *do* know is that at the time, a serial killer and grave robber named Ed Gein lived just forty miles from Bloch in Plainfield, Wisconsin. And the horrific news about Gein's killings also influenced Bloch's novel.

What do you think? Would *you* ever stay the night in a haunted motel? If you get the chance to stay at the Bates Motel, perhaps your stay will inspire you to write a frighteningly good horror novel of your own. But just remember... when you check into a haunted motel, there's no guarantee you'll *ever* check out.

## D-Mac's

Have you ever wondered what it would be like to have dinner with a ghost? Now is your chance! A restaurant named D-Mac's on Hauser Lake (about eighteen miles northwest of Coeur d'Alene) is known to be haunted by a friendly female spirit.

The building that houses the restaurant is situated over the spot where a small cabin once stood in the late 1800s. Over the years, the building has been home to a number of businesses, including a resort and a saloon, but the ghosts don't seem to mind.

One of the ghosts is a beautiful woman wearing a white dress who strolls around the dining area. Her name is Maddie. When Maddie was alive, she worked in the building and somehow ended up dead—possibly even murdered! Maddie loved to play the piano and was known to entertain visitors by singing and playing music for hours on end.

Today, her restless spirit still wanders D-Mac's and entertains guests. Although there is no piano at D-Mac's, piano music can be heard in the restaurant. And both employees and guests often report hearing the sounds of a woman humming, laughing, and singing. Maddie is a fun-loving ghost and seems to always be in a good mood. She enjoys playing small pranks on people, like moving glasses

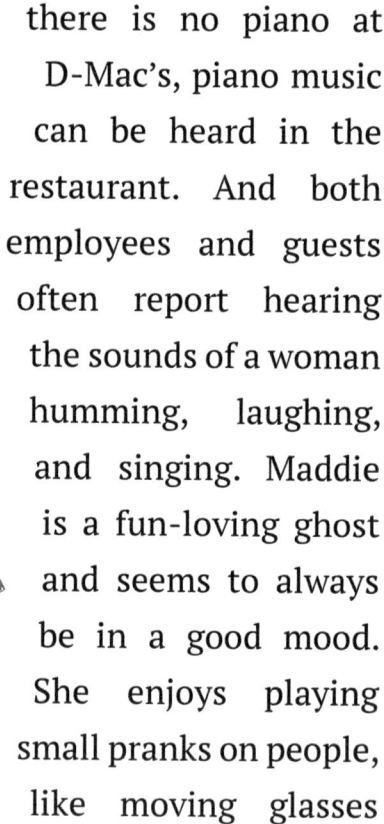

and silverware, and loves to turn lights off and on.

If you're ever visiting Hauser Lake, why not stop by D-Mac's for a nice dinner with your family—*and* a chance encounter with a friendly, piano-playing ghost!

# Part 2: Silver Valley Haunts

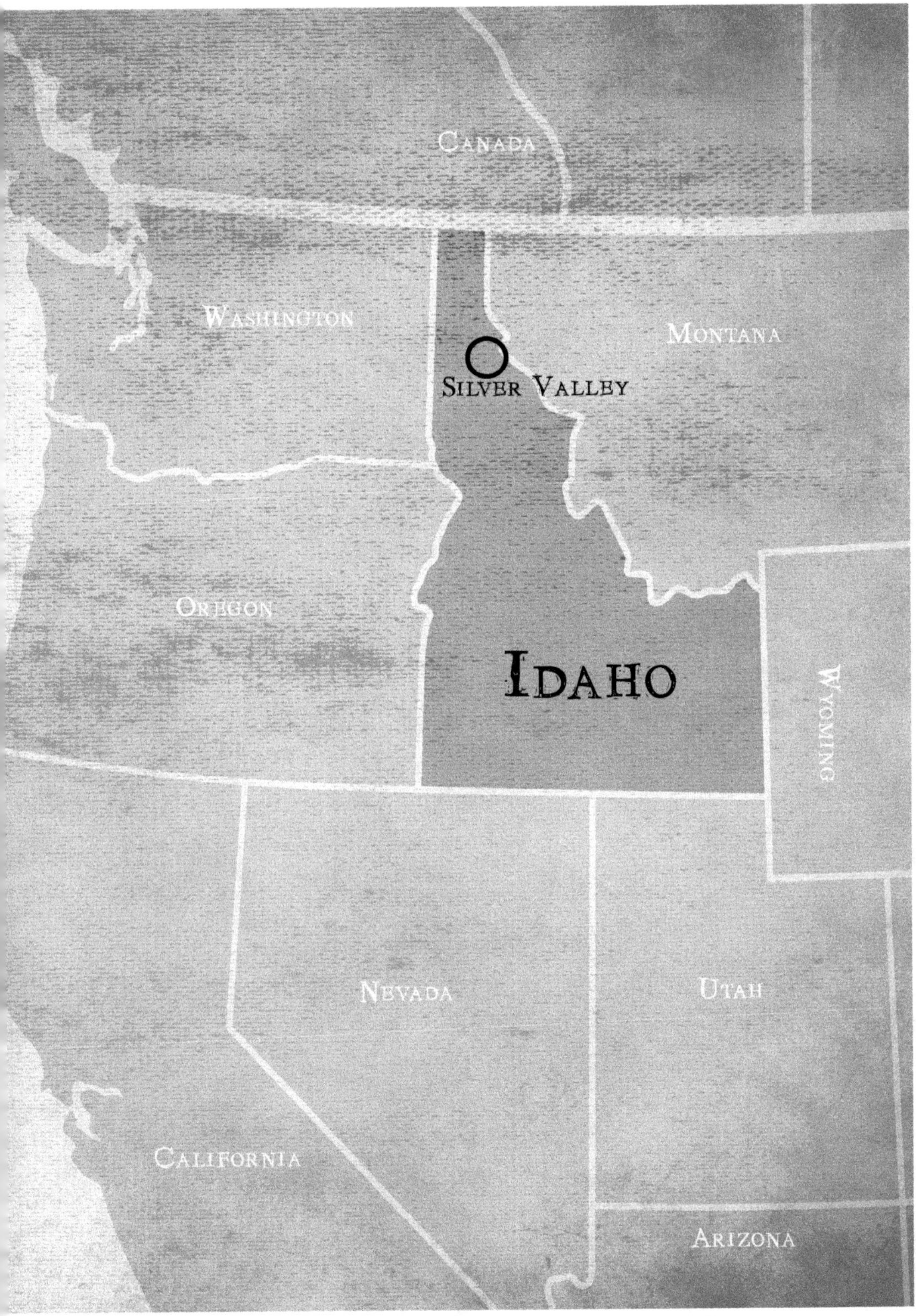
Canada
Washington
Montana
Silver Valley
Oregon
Idaho
Wyoming
Nevada
Utah
California
Arizona

**Miners in the Silver Valley in 1910**

Sacred Heart Mission church

# The Cataldo Mission

The oldest building in Idaho is the Sacred Heart Mission church in Cataldo, which is about twenty-three miles east of Coeur d'Alene. It was built by the Christian missionaries who came to the area hoping to convert the indigenous tribes. When Father Pierre-Jean DeSmet arrived in the area around 1841, he encountered the Coeur d'Alene tribe who lived there.

One of the tribe members, Circling Raven, had a vivid dream that disturbed him. The next morning, he went to his chief and said, "I saw a group of light-skinned men wearing long, black robes coming to our village. These men would bring with them a new religion that would change our lives forever."

Father DeSmet and the missionaries began building the beautiful Cataldo Mission in 1850 using local resources. Under Father DeSmet's command was Italian-born Father Ravalli, who wanted the mission to look like the cathedrals of his homeland. He supervised the Coeur d'Alene men, who, with a few simple tools, helped construct this marvelous structure.

With their help, the church on the site, known as Sacred Heart Mission church, began to take shape. The six columns adorning the front were carved from nearby trees. It is remarkable that not a single iron nail was used when building the church. The team was creative when decorating their new church since resources were very limited. They recycled tin cans into small lamp shades, created homemade wallpaper by staining old newsprint with berry juice, and colored the beams in the church a beautiful blue by crushing huckleberries into them.

It took three years to complete the spectacular church. But is it also... spectacularly *haunted*? Some visitors report feeling an almost otherworldly sense of peace

and tranquility when visiting the church. Perhaps the spirit of either Father DeSmet or Father Ravalli (or both!) still lingers around the historic building, not wanting to leave this special place, even after death.

Today the Old Mission State Park is open to the public and hosts a small cemetery, the Sacred Heart Mission church, and a beautifully restored parish house where visitors can view displayed items that missionaries used when they built the church.

THE CATALDO MISSION

If you visit Cataldo Mission and Sacred Heart Mission church, perhaps you'll catch a ghostly glimpse of some of the priests who dedicated their lives to the place. And if you do, hopefully you'll feel a sense of peace and tranquility rather than a scary, spine-tingling sensation that can only mean one thing: *RUN!*

Mining equipment in Murray

# Chapter 3

# Murray

If you head about sixty miles east of Coeur d'Alene, you come to Murray, a remote, old mining town filled with restless spirits! The town was established in 1884, two years after a man named Andrew Pritchard first discovered gold in the area. He found the gold quite by accident. He was in the area hoping to get a timber contract when, to his surprise, he stumbled upon gold instead!

The news of a gold rush in the Coeur d'Alene region quickly caught the attention of a lot of people. Before long, Murray and two smaller towns nearby, Prichard and Eagle City, were swarming with gold prospectors hoping to strike it rich. Over ten thousand people flocked to this cluster of small towns. They pitched tents and were soon building restaurants, banks, bakeries, and even a small jail. (After all, when it comes to gold, some people will do whatever it takes to strike it rich—even if that means breaking the law!)

The rumor of gold in Murray attracted two of the Wild West's most famous characters—Wyatt Earp and Calamity Jane. The notorious outlaw and adventurous horsewoman came to town in hopes of making some money off the miners. In 1884, Earp and his family settled in Eagle City and erected a huge circus tent, which they ran as the White Elephant Saloon. The Earps didn't want to pan for gold—that wasn't their style. They simply wanted to make money off the men searching for gold.

Earp maintained law and order in town and soon the locals were eager to make him the next sheriff. However, the Earps packed up their belongings and hightailed it out of town almost as quickly as they had come. There were rumors that the gunslinger was scheduled to be hanged from the nearest tree the next morning for taking over other people's claims to mines, known as mine claim jumping. No wonder Wyatt and his family hurriedly left town in the middle of the night!

Calamity Jane was a legendary frontierswoman, as well as a dramatic storyteller. She loved to have a good time, play games and cards, and gather a group of people around a campfire at night and tell outlandish stories. Always an entertainer, Jane kept everyone on the edge of their seats with her incredible tales, which ranged from scouting for the U.S. Army and riding for the Pony Express, to baking a cake that could last twenty years.

Today, there are just a few original buildings left standing in the tiny town of Murray: the Murray House Bed & Breakfast, the Sprag Pole Inn, and the Bedroom Goldmine Bar. If you ever come to Murray seeking supernatural encounters, keep in mind that each one of these buildings is known to have its own special ghosts. From innkeepers to prospectors and even a ghostly little girl, they all seem to be former citizens of Murray—people who loved the town so much in life, that they never wanted to leave.

## A Ghost in Search of Gold

One of the best places to eat in Murray is the Bedroom Goldmine Bar. Popular for its pizza, burgers, and heavenly smelling garlic breadsticks, it's also one of the best places in town to spot a ghost! Believed to be a prospector who doesn't want anyone to get their hands on his gold, this ghost likes to open and close doors and play tricks on the staff and customers.

Originally built in 1884 by E.W. Burten, the building once housed a bakery and a general store. After changing ownership many times over the years, Chris and Lucille Christopherson purchased the building in 1967 and turned it into a tavern. Chris had always dreamed of finding gold, and while Lucille tended bar, he soon began digging in the back room of the building. Chris thought that since it was one of the last remaining original buildings in town, there might just be gold beneath the floors. And guess what? There *was*! After years of digging, he had created a thirty-four-foot-deep mine shaft where he was lucky enough to find a large gold nugget—one of the largest ever found in the Coeur d'Alene's. Chris continued to dig until he was in his 80s, although he never found another nugget as big as the first one. Many locals think that the

ghost haunting the Bedroom Goldmine Bar is Chris, still searching for more precious gold.

Other people say the ghost is Frank Grebil. Frank's wife, Leila, is the niece of Chris Christopherson, and she inherited the tavern from her uncle. For many years, Frank and Leila searched for gold nuggets just as Chris had, but they were never as lucky.

While alive, Frank's favorite place to sit in the bar was at a stool directly in front of a large wooden beam, where he would rest his back. Though he died in 2000, many continue to feel his presence in the building to this day. When the front door flies open for no apparent reason, the customers all turn their heads in curiosity. The waitresses just laugh and say, "Oh, it's probably Frank."

Could Frank's spirit still be haunting his old restaurant? Is he the ghost that plays pranks? Or could it be *both* Chris and Frank still hanging around, neither one willing to leave the town and tavern they loved so much? With all the spooky activity inside these walls, it certainly seems possible! People have felt sudden drafts of ice-cold air, seen invisible hands move objects, and smelled hints of cigarette smoke, even though no one is allowed to smoke inside!

If you ever get the chance to visit Murray, why not drop by the Bedroom Goldmine Bar? Perhaps you'll be lucky enough to encounter the ghosts of Frank and Chris while there. (Remember, when a glass moves toward you across a table all by itself, don't be scared. It's probably just one of them trying to serve you a soda.) In the back room, the mining shaft that Chris dug is on display under a thick layer of glass. You can peer down into the ground and see where he spent all those years searching for gold. And maybe, just *maybe*, you'll even see his ghost peering back up at you!

## The Ghost on the Stairs

The 1884 Murray House bed-and-breakfast (a place to stay that offers guests lodging and breakfast) is another one of the few original buildings still remaining from the town's earliest days. Many people claim to have seen the ghostly image of the house's original owner, Adam Aulbach. His spirit likes to appear inside a mysterious cloud of smoke on the stairs.

Aulbach built the house in 1884 when he came to Murray to set up his printing shop. He founded the local newspaper, the *Idaho Sun*, and was so involved in everything that he became known as the pillar of the community. Locals even called him the Grand Old Man of Murray! He did everything he could to promote and boost the

small town, and he lived in the very same home he had built until he died there peacefully in 1933. To this day, his spirit continues to roam the halls and bedrooms, looking over the house as lovingly as he did when he was alive.

The current owners, Larry and Sandy Hammer, have seen Aulbach's ghost many times. They sometimes smell cigar smoke, even though guests are not allowed to smoke inside. Once, Sandy was taking photographs of the building for their website. She suddenly felt a cold chill and the strange sensation that someone was watching her. When she turned around, however, there was nobody in sight. A little spooked, Sandy moved to the base of the staircase and continued taking pictures. Imagine her shock when she looked up and saw an eerie cloud of smoke rolling toward her down the stairs! For a moment, she was terrified that something had caught fire in one of the rooms on the second floor. She rushed upstairs past the smoke and quickly investigated, but she saw no sign of fire anywhere. If there was no fire, then where had the bizarre smoke come from?

When Sandy came back downstairs, the strange smoke had mysteriously vanished. She was left scratching her head, with no clue what had caused this strange phenomenon.

Later that evening, as she was sorting through the photographs she had taken, Sandy froze. Gazing back at her in one of the pictures, clear as day, was the image of Adam Aulbach's face in the smoke! She did a double take. Were her eyes playing tricks on her? She looked again, squinting hard, but there was no mistaking it. His large nose, thick mustache, and deep-set eyes were all visible in the smoke!

Sandy and her husband Larry were baffled. How—and *why*—had Adam Aulbach's ghost appeared to them? What was he trying to tell Sandy? Was he simply happy she and her husband were taking such great care of his home? Did he approve of the recent updates they had made? After a time, the couple decided that Adam had simply been saying hello. Considering he'd once been such an important part of the community, it made sense that he was still hanging around. And after all, like Dorothy says in *The Wizard of Oz*, "There's no place like home."

In addition to Aulbach's ghost, visitors sometimes see the specter of a small girl in the upstairs rooms. She is a shy, quiet spirit. Though her identity is a bit of a mystery, some believe she is Adam Aulbach's daughter, Ruth. Does Ruth hang around the Murray house because her father's spirit still resides there, too? Possibly! Ruth and her father were very close and perhaps they remain so—even in death.

If you ever stay at the 1884 Murray House bed-and-breakfast, you too may catch a glimpse of this ghostly father-daughter duo. Maybe Mr. Aulbach will peek his head around a corner to say "Hello" to you! Or, you may see Ruth as she sits in a rocking chair, patiently waiting for someone to read her a story.

## Haunted Antiques

The Sprag Pole Inn and Museum was once a hardware store carrying mining equipment, lumber, nails, tools, and odds and ends for locals. In 1885, the building was turned into a stagecoach stop where people could catch a horse-drawn wagon or buggy ride into Wallace, Eagle City, or Prichard.

In 1933, Walt and Bess Almquist bought the building and turned it into a restaurant. Nearly forty years later, in 1970, the couple began collecting strange and unusual antiques and curios. Over time, Walt created a museum where their collection of old and rare oddities remain on display to this day for people to enjoy. Well worth the visit, one can wander around the rooms and see all kinds of artifacts from the past. The museum gives guests a look at how things were in the "olden days."

For example, do you know how people made butter centuries ago? Or how they made their clothes? Any idea how they lighted or heated their homes before things like electricity or furnaces had been invented? Have you ever seen a telegraph machine? (Have you even heard the word *telegraph* before?) Long ago—way before iPhones, texting, and FaceTime—people had to rely on the services of a telegraph operator to relay messages back and forth. It may be hard to believe, but simple tasks like making coffee, washing and ironing clothes, or even calling friends or family to say

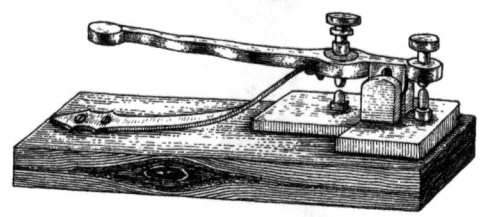

hello were *very* different just a few decades ago compared to today.

Not only does the museum house this collection of strange items, it is *also* said to

house the ghosts of the people who once owned these old and unusual artifacts. What do you think? Do you believe spirits can linger with their personal belongings after they have died? Some people who've visited the museum report items being moved, icy-cold drafts, phantom footsteps, and whispers from beyond the grave! Perhaps these ghosts loved these items so much in life, they can't seem to let go? Or maybe they want their belongings back, so they can use them ... forever?

# Chapter 4

# Kellogg

### A Donkey and a Dream

One of the strangest stories told in the Silver Valley is of a donkey who found the largest silver veins in the Coeur d'Alene Mountains!

In 1884, a man named Noah Kellogg (after whom the town of Kellogg is named) came to the area with just five dollars in his pocket, a few items of clothing, and his bedroll. He was a good man and many people liked him, but his finances were in pretty poor shape. Kellogg was hoping to strike it rich during the gold rush. But unfortunately, that didn't happen.

Kellogg needed to find work, so he took on odd jobs for people here and there—sometimes for nothing more than a piece of bacon or a stale biscuit. His circumstances were looking bleak, and he was soon penniless.

Then one night as he slept on his hard cot in a cold tent, Noah had a vivid dream. He was a firm believer in dreams and visions. This particular night, he dreamed that a nearby mountain had opened up and inside were several large veins of silver and gold. He awoke with a start and wondered: Was it just a dream or a sign from God?

Noah was down to his last penny. He did not even own a donkey anymore, but after his vision, he was confident that his dream could become reality. He walked back into town and borrowed a donkey and a few dollars from friends and headed off into the mountains. There he set up his tent, tied the donkey to a tree, and crawled into his tent. When he woke up the next morning, he discovered his borrowed donkey was gone! The animal had wandered off sometime during the night.

Frantic, Noah began searching for the lost donkey. Soon he noticed little tufts of donkey hair caught in bushes and on trees, so he followed them in hopes they would lead him to his misbehaved donkey. He finally caught up to

the critter, but it was on the other side of a creek. The donkey was staring straight at something in the grass and refused to look up. Noah called and called for the donkey, but the donkey continued to ignore him. Frustrated, Noah plodded through the water to retrieve his stubborn animal.

When he got to his donkey's side, he spotted what the donkey was staring at—a huge vein of lead and silver!

Excited about his discovery, Noah borrowed some more money from his friends and began to mine the vein. But he was about to discover something even *more* exciting—he had stumbled upon one of the biggest silver finds in history! The mine, called the Bunker Hill Mine, sold in 1885 for $1.5 million, and by 1910, it had profits of over $12 million! Noah Kellogg had gone from penniless to one of the richest men around.

And all this fortune because Noah had believed in his dream... and, of course, had a little help from a stubborn donkey.

## The Sunshine Mine Disaster

The tragic story of how ninety-one men lost their lives one horrible day will be forever etched in Idaho's history. The Sunshine Mine had been producing silver since 1904 and had made many men very wealthy. But on May 2, 1972, wealth meant nothing to those involved in the disaster.

On that day, a disastrous fire broke out in the Sunshine Mine, trapping 173 men deep underground. Lethal carbon monoxide poured into the tunnels, and dark, thick smoke blocked most of the exits. Panic ensued. Those above ground began praying for the men's safety. Those below ground began praying to be rescued.

Miraculously, eighty-two men made it out of the mine alive. However, after several hours of rescue efforts, it began to look grim for the miners still underground. For days, there seemed to be little hope, with many men succumbing to carbon monoxide poisoning. Yet on May 9—175 long hours later—as rescuers were bringing up the bodies of those who had died, they found two miners still alive.

Today, a memorial stands proudly near the site of the mine in honor of the men who tragically lost their lives. It is the statue of a miner whose helmet shines a continually

burning light in remembrance of those who perished. Some say they have seen the ghosts of these miners near the disaster site. Others claim to have seen the sorrowful spirits of the women who continue to mourn the loss of their husbands, sons, and brothers standing near the statue.

Located just off I-90, you can visit the memorial to pay your respects to those who died in the Sunshine Mine disaster. And perhaps, while you're there, you will also see the spirit of someone whose life was touched by the tragedy that day in 1972.

## Missing Gold

In 1883, a young man named Edward Cornelius had gotten wind of the Coeur d'Alene gold rush and decided to cash in on it. Not by prospecting, but by purchasing real estate. Edward and a friend made the long trip from

Montana to Idaho on horseback, carrying with them the gold they would use to buy property and a couple of donkeys. However, when they arrived in Coeur d'Alene, they discovered that the stories they'd heard had been greatly exaggerated. And, in fact, there was no big gold rush after all.

Now what were they to do? They were hundreds of miles away from home and had no idea what their next step would be. They had planned on investing their gold in local real estate, hoping to resell it to lucky miners who had struck it rich. Since that plan had gone up in smoke, the men found themselves not knowing what to do.

Word got out that the pair were in possession of a very large amount of gold, and local robbers began plotting how to steal it. Edward and his pal were nervous that someone was going to murder them and run off with all their gold.

So, the two friends hatched a plan: they decided to bury the gold and retrieve it later. (In 1883, many people didn't trust banks to look after their money.)

The only thing they had on them at the time that could withstand the harsh elements of an Idaho winter was a cast iron Dutch oven. The men chose a flat spot of land located within a triangle of trees—two pines and one fir—so they would remember where their treasure was hidden. Then they put all of their gold and valuables inside the Dutch oven and buried it. The men felt satisfied that their fortune would be secure until they could return to retrieve it.

But bad luck intervened. A large fire broke out in the area and burned down all the trees! Their tree markers were gone! The men returned to the approximate spot of their buried fortune, but despite much digging, they were never able to find it. For over thirty years, the men searched tirelessly in the hopes of retrieving their lost gold.

Since that time, the area has been developed, and hundreds of homes, stores, parking lots, and streets have covered most of the area where the gold would have been buried. But that hasn't stopped Edward and his friend from looking for their buried treasure. Their wandering ghosts can still be seen every now and then searching for their lost fortune.

Maybe someday some lucky gardener will be digging in their backyard and strike something hard and metallic with their shovel. Perhaps when they dig farther to investigate, they will discover a rusty, old Dutch oven, and be amazed when they open it up to find *millions* of dollars' worth of gold! (They'd better watch out for two treasure hunting ghosts, in that case!)

Cornelius and his buddy were not the only men who thought it was a good idea to bury their fortune in the Silver Valley. Butch Cassidy, the famous bank and train robber, and his gang (known as the Wild Bunch) also buried some of their stolen money somewhere between Spokane Falls and Wallace. The only clues they recorded were that the money was buried by an old stagecoach road and near a river next to a beaver dam. So far, nobody has ever been able to find it, though lots of people have tried. What do you think? Would you risk a lifetime of spooky spirits haunting you for a chance at finding centuries-old, buried gold? Grab your flashlight and your shovel if the answer is yes... but don't say we didn't warn you about the ghosts!

# CHAPTER 5

# Wallace

The old mining town of Wallace, located forty-eight miles east of Coeur d'Alene, has more stories of murders and mayhem than anywhere else in the Silver Valley! In fact, almost every building here is haunted by a ghost or two.

Founded in 1884, Wallace has survived more than its fair share of natural disasters. It's also seen a multitude of murders, robberies, riots, gun duels, and horrific fires and floods. (No wonder it's home to so many ghosts!) Going back more than a hundred years, Wallace holds the record as the world's largest silver producer, making it the richest mining town anywhere. Locals have often claimed to see the spirits of cowboys and miners wandering the streets. It's hard to know who these spirits are, but they obviously wanted to stick around in Wallace for a reason, even after death. Maybe it's the beauty of the surrounding Bitterroot Mountains, the fun of the old wild West, or all that shiny silver. Either way, it's no wonder the ghosts never want to leave.

## A Movie Star and Memories

Even the ghost of a legendary movie star is said to gracefully stroll the streets in Wallace! A glamorous actress named Lana Turner, who was a Hollywood star in the 1940s and 1950s, was born in Wallace. But once she moved to California, her off-screen life read like a movie script filled with rumors and scandals. Many believe that after Turner's death in 1995, her spirit returned to Wallace to get away from the whirlwind of Hollywood.

Even though Lana Turner had a successful film career, she was unlucky in love and married eight times. Eight weddings might sound a little scandalous, but Turner's love life made the biggest headlines in 1958, when her fourteen-year-old daughter stabbed her ill-tempered mobster boyfriend, Johnny Stompanato, to death.

Lana's childhood home in Wallace is currently being remodeled after many years of sitting vacant. It's said that Lana's ghost now roams the streets of town. Could it be that Lana has returned to the town where she grew up, longing for a simpler time? Perhaps she's left behind the eternal stresses and strains of Hollywood to seek out a quiet, more peaceful life back in her small hometown? No one knows for sure, but one thing is certain: if you see the ghostly silhouette of a glamorous movie star strolling down Cedar and Bank streets in Wallace, you can bet it is Lana Turner!

## The Ghost of Mournful Maggie

One of the saddest ghost stories from Silver Valley involves a young woman who fell in love with a married man. Her tragic spirit still roams the historic halls and rooms of the magnificent, historic Jameson Hotel on 6th Street in Wallace.

The sturdy brick hotel was built in 1907

by Theodore Jameson to replace a wooden building that had stood on the same spot. It, like many other buildings in town, had burned to the ground in a horrible fire in 1890. Inside the three-story Jameson Hotel, you can admire the old mahogany staircases, fabulous archways, gorgeous woodwork, and tin ceilings. All of that, along with the antique furnishings, give the feeling that time has stood still at the hotel.

There is a local legend about a girl (known only as Maggie) who used to stay at the hotel in the 1920s. She would travel by train from St. Louis, Missouri, and wait there for her beau (or boyfriend) to meet her. He had promised to marry her and that they would start a life together. Maggie worked odd jobs in Wallace to pay for her room while she waited for her beau. But one time he never showed up. Heartbroken, Maggie left Wallace and never returned. Did she meet someone else and fall in love? Did she die of a broken heart? Or did she meet an even more tragic fate?

No real records can be found of Maggie's stay at the hotel, but the people of Wallace have passed this story down for almost one hundred years. In the room where it's said she stayed at the Jameson, people see objects move on their own, lights turn on and off by themselves, and even doors mysteriously locking and unlocking. Sometimes the impression of a head on a pillow forms in Maggie's old room, even when no one has slept there!

Once, it sounded as if there was a party in full swing on the third floor—everything from music to glasses clinking to toilets flushing could be heard. But when the hotel manager ran up the stairs to see what was going on, he found all the doors locked and the rooms silent. It didn't make any sense—he knew what he had heard—and yet no one was up there! Because of her sad story, it seems odd that Maggie would be holding a ghostly party in her old room. And paranormal investigators concluded that another ghost named Ollie was probably responsible for all the late-night festivities.

Indeed, Ollie is famous not only for his rowdy ways but also for giving plenty of ghostly hugs. Many people claim to have felt his phantom arms wrap around their bodies in a sweet, but definitely eerie, expression of love.

If you do get a change to stay at the Jameson Hotel, perhaps you'll experience one of the ghosts there. Will it be tragic Maggie, or party boy Ollie?

# A "Sweet" Ghost

One ghost who haunts Wallace is the original owner of the Sweets Hotel, which stands next to the Jameson Hotel on 6th Street. Originally from Pennsylvania, Lewis Sweet came to Wallace in 1891 with just the clothes on his back, one horse, and two dimes in his pocket.

But that did not deter Lewis. Through hard work and determination, he worked his way up and was soon running one of the biggest hotels in Wallace!

Lewis Sweet was one of the kindest men in town and always liked to help those less fortunate than he. He enjoyed participating in local parades and events and was known around town as being a good card player. When Lewis Sweet died in 1929, the entire town mourned his passing.

Although the Sweets Hotel has fallen into disrepair, many people in Wallace would love to see someone bring it back to its former glory. In the meantime, locals and employees hear hushed voices and strange knocks, see apparitions on the stairs, and smell perfume and cigar smoke. Is it the ghost of Mr. Lewis Sweet himself making sure that his hotel is being looked after?

Another possible ghost in the Sweets Hotel is a man who went missing in 1906. His name was M.B. Rice, and he was a salesman from Spokane, Washington. He was traveling alone over the Thanksgiving holiday and stayed at one of the other hotels in Wallace.

But though Mr. Rice checked into his room ... he never checked out!

Even more mysterious is that his body was never found and no one ever came looking for him. It's as if Mr. Rice vanished into thin air!

Some speculate that M.B. Rice's spirit haunts both the Jameson and Sweets hotels. What do you think? Perhaps he's hoping he can finally check out. Or maybe he's seeking justice for his untimely and mysterious death!

## The Ryan Hotel

The Ryan Hotel was built in 1903 and is one of the few original buildings in town that survived the Big Burn of 1910. That horrific fire destroyed three million acres of private and public land across Idaho, Montana, and Washington.

But this building is also special for another reason: one of the most active ghosts in Wallace calls the Ryan Hotel home. In life, her name was Miss Dorothy Montgomery. She taught third grade at the local school and lived at the Ryan Hotel for forty-three years.

Those who knew Miss Dorothy considered her to be a real lady. She was kind, well-dressed, loved teaching children, and was always on time. Though she could at times be stern (apparently, Miss Dorothy once flunked an entire class!), she was known overall to be a friendly and considerate guest. So, it's no surprise she continues to be a friendly and considerate ghost!

Sometimes Miss Dorothy surprises the current owner, Donna, with helpful hints. Once, a guest accidentally left their laptop in the room. Donna was on her way to another part of the hotel, but she suddenly got a strong feeling to go check the room the guest had just left. As soon as Donna entered the room, she spotted the laptop that had been left behind and was luckily able hand it over before the guest drove off.

Another time, guests saw what appeared to be a ghostly pilot from another era walk down the hall and into a room! When a ghost hunter listened to recordings made inside that room, they heard the hushed voice of a man, and the word "flight" appeared on the device's screen.

Guests also report seeing the ghost of a little girl bouncing around the Ryan Hotel. No one is sure who she is, but she is always happy and energetic. She likes to move things around, and her delightful laughter can often be heard echoing through the halls.

A ghostly couple sometimes appears in one of the back rooms, apparently enjoying their stay at the hotel. It's thought they may be James Watson and J. Poucher, who were married at the Ryan Hotel in 1912. They don't show themselves regularly, however, so it's possible they only come back to the Ryan for special occasions and anniversaries.

The ghosts of several unknown men also come and go at the hotel. It's a mystery who they are. Perhaps former guests, one of the previous owners, or the card players who took part in a big poker game at the hotel way back in 1906?

Today, the Ryan Hotel stands as a symbol of the area's history. Stepping inside the friendly lobby is like stepping back in time. The rooms contain many original features and antique furniture. Plus, the hotel is always extremely clean and tidy. (No wonder Miss Dorothy doesn't want to leave!) Though the identities of some of its ghosts remain a mystery, the Ryan Hotel is obviously home to plenty of guests who've decided to never check out. And who knows, it's such a warm and welcoming place, perhaps the Ryan may end up being home to even *more* ghostly guests.

Only time will tell.

## The Brooks Hotel

The historic Brooks Hotel in downtown Wallace is a favorite place for locals and tourists. Built in 1905, the two-story brick building has been home to various businesses over the years. Once a hospital, it has also been a department store, a dry goods store, and an office building. Today, Rachel and Emily, a mother-daughter team, run the hotel, bar, and restaurant. And their extensive remodeling has perked up a ghost or two!

At times, guests hear the sound of phantom footsteps walking up and down the hallways—but when they open the door, no one is there! Rachel and Emily aren't sure who, exactly, may be haunting their hotel. Perhaps it was a nurse or doctor from way back when the building was a hospital, hoping to find more

patients to attend to. Or maybe it's a former store owner who likes to keep a watchful eye on his merchandise? Perhaps it's simply a guest who has decided to spend eternity at their favorite hotel?

The truth is, nobody really knows. Because when it comes to ghostly guests, anything is possible! So if you and your family ever stay at the Brooks Hotel, be alert. With ghostly guests regularly wandering the halls, you may very well bump into one!

## A Phantom Fireman

The Big Burn of 1910 was one of the largest forest fires in American history. Tragically, seventy-eight firefighters lost their lives battling the flames. There is an area marked near Wallace where a brave U.S. Forest Service Ranger, Edward Pulaski, saved the lives of his team by forcing them (and a couple of horses!)

into a hillside tunnel. By doing this, Pulaski was able to limit the exposure his men and animals endured during the horrendous fire.

Pulaski was supervising crews on the west of Placer Creek, about five miles south of Wallace, when the fire suddenly got out of control, overwhelming the crew. He knew that his men would all die from smoke inhalation or be burned alive if he didn't act fast. Twelve men had already died at Big Creek, three more at Pine Creek, and another twenty-eight at Seltzer Creek.

Pulaski knew the area well, and he led his team to an old mining tunnel that was part of the Nicholson Mine site. He then hung a thick blanket (which the men had soaked in a nearby creek) over the opening of the tunnel to keep out as much smoke and heat as possible.

Inside the tunnel, some men challenged Pulaski's orders, but Pulaski was unyielding. "I will shoot *any* man who tries to leave the safety of this tunnel!" he threatened.

The temperature was so hot inside the tunnel that the men's faces and hands were becoming blistered—even behind the water-soaked blanket. They had to push their faces into the mud to try to limit the burns.

Within a short time, all the men had passed out from the heat and smoke. During the night, one man was able to make his way out of the tunnel and head into Wallace to notify anyone left in town about the firefighters still trapped inside the tunnel.

A rescue team followed the firefighter's path back to the tunnel, and they discovered that, miraculously, only five men and the two horses had died.

Many firefighting policies were changed because of the Big Burn, and a new type of axe was invented and named after Edward Pulaski. A hiking trail outside of Wallace is also named after Pulaski and, in 1921, a memorial was erected at Nine Mile Cemetery.

Ghost hunters tell stories of glowing orbs, strange noises, and apparitions at the Nine Mile Cemetery. Are these the spirits of the men who perished in the massive fire? Some people claim to have seen the ghost of a man walking near the tunnel on the Pulaski Trail. Perhaps it's Edward Pulaski, returning to make sure that his men are safe?

## Ghosts on Stage

Another location in town that has a lot of ghostly activity is the old 6th Street Theater. Once a wallpaper and paint store, the theater is the oldest-standing wooden structure in the town's Historic District.

But be warned: if you go to see a play or attend a community event at the theater, you may be more scared than entertained. That's because mysterious shadowy figures abound in the theater!

Many old theaters are haunted by former actors and actresses who don't want to leave the stage. And the 6th Street Theater is no exception. Employees often see objects move on their own and hear phantom voices inside the building. Upstairs, a strange, lingering scent is often present. The stage overhead lights flicker on and off, and the odor of cigarette smoke wafts through the air. (Smoking is not permitted in the building).

However, many believe that a female ghost often seen in the theater is not a former actress but a former *owner* of the building, named Delores Arnold. Although Delores eventually moved to Reno, Nevada, some say her spirit lingers at the old theater she lovingly called her home for so many years.

If you visit the 6th Street Theater, maybe you'll be lucky enough to see one of the spirits who resides there make a ghostly curtain call... happily taking their final bows, forever.

## Nine Mile Cemetery

Nine Mile Cemetery is a vast, rolling graveyard that seems to go on forever. Dating back to the 1880s, countless souls have been buried there. Many of Wallace's prominent citizens now reside for all eternity among the cemetery's towering trees, mossy tombstones, and wrought iron fences.

Many locals and tourists claim to have seen odd flashing lights and bright floating orbs. They've caught strange voices on tape recorders and reported other bizarre phenomena at the cemetery. With so many souls haunting the area, it is hard to pin down exactly who it might be!

But one ghost, in particular, might be responsible for haunting the grounds—a man named Herman Rossi, who used to be Wallace's mayor.

Back in 1916, a murder occurred in one of the most elegant and prominent hotels in Wallace, the Samuel's Hotel. The grand structure is no longer part of Wallace's landscape, but back in the day, it was truly amazing. The spectacular five-story hotel towered above every other building in downtown Wallace. Built in 1908 by Henry Floyd Samuels, the elegant hotel soon became the showpiece of the county. Located on the corner of 7th and Cedar streets, it boasted 150 rooms (with both hot and cold running water!), intricately carved staircases, and a fantastic iron, birdcage-style elevator.

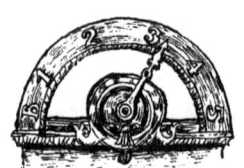

One day, Herman Rossi returned from a business trip and discovered that his wife had been going out with another man while he was away. He was outraged! Herman grabbed his revolver and marched from his house on Cedar Street to Samuel's Hotel. There he found his wife's friend, Clarence "Gabe" Dahlquist, relaxing with some buddies in the hotel lobby.

After hitting Dahlquist on the head with the gun several times, Rossi then pointed it at him and fired. Rossi marched out of the hotel and headed to his office, trying to gain his composure.

Two of Rossi's friends followed him.

"You know you shot him, right?" one of the men asked Rossi.

"If I did, I didn't mean to, and I am sorry," was all Rossi said.

Doctors rushed Dahlquist to Providence Hospital in Wallace, but he died the next day.

Though Rossi later stood trial for Dahlquist's murder, he was acquitted (or found innocent) after only one hour of debate among the jury members.

Rossi and his wife Mabel divorced, and Mabel was never seen again. Where she fled to remains a mystery to this day.

The grand Samuel's Hotel fell into disrepair and was sadly torn down in 1974. Today, a green space called the Harry F. Magnuson Park is located where the hotel once stood.

Many believe the ghost of Herman Rossi still haunts the cemetery, remorseful for what he did to poor Dahlquist. Others believe it is the ghost of Mabel they see walking late at night, still furious at Rossi for killing her friend in cold blood. Perhaps it is even Dahlquist himself, angry at Rossi for taking his life at such a young age.

The mystery of whose spirits roam Nine Mile Cemetery remains just that—a *mystery*. Of the three suspected ghosts, whose voice do *you* think can still be heard whispering in the breeze? Or do you believe it is all three... still arguing among the tombstones and the trees?

# A Ghostly Goodbye

Do you think ghosts truly exist or are a figment of our imaginations?

Whether you live in Coeur d'Alene or are just passing through, you are sure to have a spookily fun time learning about all the ghosts and haunted places in northern Idaho. There are plenty of them in Coeur d'Alene and the Silver Valley. *Happy ghost hunting!*

**Deborah Cuyle** has written almost a dozen books on haunted places and towns, and lived for several years in her *own* haunted house in Wallace, Idaho. She loves swapping ghostly tales with her family and friends while nestled around a bonfire. Visit her on Facebook (www.facebook.com/CuyleBooks/) to learn more!

Check out some of the other *Spooky America* titles available now!

*Spooky America* was adapted from the creeptastic *Haunted America* series for adults. *Haunted America* explores historical haunts in cities and regions across America. Here's more from the original *Ghosts of Coeur d'Alene and the Silver Valley* author, Deborah Cuyle:

www.ingramcontent.com/pod-product-compliance
Lightning Source LLC
Chambersburg PA
CBHW070347100426
42812CB00005B/1451